Wonders

Program Authors

Diane August

Donald R. Bear

Janice A. Dole

Jana Echevarria

Douglas Fisher

David Francis

Vicki Gibson

Jan Hasbrouck

Margaret Kilgo

Jay McTighe

Scott G. Paris

Timothy Shanahan

Josefina V. Tinajero

Mc
Graw
Hill
Education

Cover and Title pages: Nathan Love

www.mheonline.com/readingwonders

Copyright © 2017 McGraw-Hill Education

Send all inquiries to:
McGraw-Hill Education
2 Penn Plaza
New York, NY 10121

ISBN: 978-0-07-678539-1
MHID: 0-07-678539-4

Printed in the United States of America.

2 3 4 5 6 7 8 9 RMN 20 19 18 17 16

Unit 6 Weather for all Seasons

The Big Idea: How do weather and seasons affect us?

(t) Ingram Publishing; (c) Cathi Mingus; (b) Danial Howarth

Essential Question
How are the seasons different?

Go Digital!

Seasons Change!

Talk About It

What season is it?

Say the name of each picture.

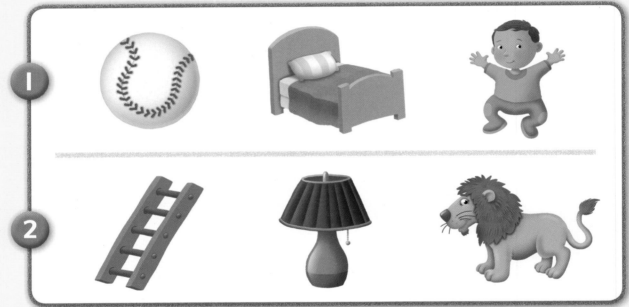

1

2

Read each word.

3 **bat**   **bed**   **bib**   **bit**

4 **let**   **lip**   **lab**   **lit**

is   **little**

Fall **is** a beautiful season.

The **little** bugs are cute.

Is It Hot?

Ben **is** a **little** cat.
It is a bit hot.

It is hot, hot, hot.
We see a fin!

Deb can hit with a bat.
Deb can hit a lot!

Let Rob sip, sip, sip!

Lin is not a bit hot.
Lin can hop on top!

13

A red hat is on it.
I set the hat on top.

It is not a bit hot!
Hop a lot if it is not hot!

Write About the Text

Pages 8–15

Zoe

I answered the prompt: **Did the author do a good job of showing what fall and winter are like?**

Student Model: *Opinion*

I think the author does a good job of showing fall.
I see different colored leaves falling.
Rob sips something warm.

Topic
My sentences tell how the author showed what fall is like.

My Feelings
I used how I felt to
form my opinion.

I like the way the author

shows winter.

I see a funny snowman!

I see children wearing

warm coats and playing

in the snow!

Grammar

The word
coats is
a **plural
noun.**

Your Turn

In your opinion,
does the author
do a good job
of showing what
spring and summer
are like?

Go Digital!
Write your response online.
Use your editing checklist.

17

Essential Question

What happens in different kinds of weather?

Go Digital!

It's Raining Cats and Dogs!

Ariel Skelley/Blend Images/Getty Images

COLLABORATE

Talk About It

What can you do
on a rainy day?

Phonics

Kk

Say the name of each picture.

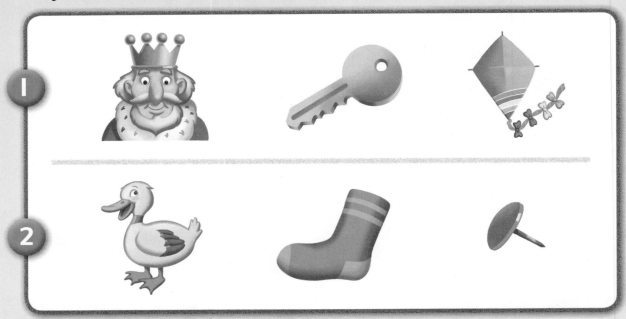

1

2

Read each word.

3 **kit** **Kim** **kid** **kick**

4 **rock** **back** **deck** **lock**

she

was

She can kick the ball.

Monday **was** a hot day!

Kim and Nan

Kim had a lot to pack.
She **was** a kid on the go.

Cathi Mingus

Nan sat on a big rock.
Kim sat on a little rock.

Cathi Mingus

Kim was hot, hot, hot.
Kim had to sip a bit.

Cathi Mingus

Kim had a red sack.
Kim fed a lot.

Nan and Kim sat and sat.
It was not a bit hot!

Kim ran back.
Nan ran back.

Kim has a red pack.
Kim is a kid on the go!

Kim and Nan

Pages 22–29

Write About the Text

Luis

I responded to the prompt: **Use dialogue to have Kim's friend ask about her day. Have Kim respond.**

Student Model: *Narrative Text*

"How was your day?"
asked Jan.

"It was a great day, Jan!"
said Kim.

Details
I used picture details to figure out how Kim feels.

"I fed the seeds to the birds.
The birds enjoyed eating
the seeds."

Grammar

Jan is a **proper noun** that names a person.

"What else did you do?" asked Jan.

"I took pictures of Nan with my camera," said Kim.

Dialogue
I wrote what Kim and Jan said to each other.

Your Turn

COLLABORATE

Tell what Kim and Jan might say to each other about Kim's next adventure. Use dialogue.

Go Digital!
Write your response online.
Use your editing checklist.

31

Essential Question

How can you stay safe in bad weather?

Go Digital!

COLLABORATE

Talk About It

How would you describe this weather?

Jeff Hunter/The Image Bank/Getty Images

Lightning Strikes!

Review Letter Sounds

Say the name of each picture.

Read each word.

3 **fan**   **hen**   **rock**   **hat**

4 **lab**   **led**   **kick**   **rib**

Nathan Jarvis

Review Words

Read the words and sentences.

1 my   are   he   was

2 is   little   she   with

3 **My** friend Nick **was** **with** me.

4 **She** and I **are** drawing.

5 **He** **is** a **little** dog.

Mack and Ben

Daniel Howarth

Pit, pat, pit, pat, pit, pat!
Mack ran **with** Ben.

Mack **was** a bit sad.
Ben hid in a **little** bed.

Daniel Howarth

Mom fed Mack and Ben.
She had a hot, hot ham.

Daniel Howarth

Daniel Howarth

Tick, tock, tick, tock!
Mack and Ben sat and sat.

Mack did not hit.
He did not kick.

Daniel Howarth

Ben can pack a bag.
Mack can pack a tan bat.

Daniel Howarth

Let Mack and Ben go.
Mack and Ben **are** back!

Daniel Howarth

Write About the Text

Pages 36–43

Paula

I responded to the prompt: **Write about what Ben and Mack might say to each other about the weather.**

Student Model: *Narrative Text*

"Mack, I'm afraid of the storm," says Ben.

"There are so many dark clouds," says Mack.

"The sun will never come out," says Ben.

Clues
I used the picture to figure out that it is stormy outside.

Grammar
Clouds is a plural **noun** that names a thing.

44

"The rain looks like it's stopping. The sun is coming out!" says Mack.

"We can play again!" say Mack and Ben!

Dialogue
I told what Ben and Mack say to each other.

Your Turn COLLABORATE

What might Ben and Mack say about what they can do now that the weather has cleared up? Write two pages.

Go Digital!
Write your response online.
Use your editing checklist.

45